LUTHER KING, JR.

and the

Struggle for Civil Rights

Dennis Fertig

Boston, Massachusetts
Chandler, Arizona
Glenview, Illinois
Upper Saddle River, New Jersey

Illustrations

Opener, 1, 3, 4, 6, 7, 8, 9, 10, 11, 13, 15 Bandelin-Dacey.

Photographs

Every effort has been made to secure permission and provide appropriate credit for photographic material.
The publisher deeply regrets any omission and pledges to correct errors called to its attention in subsequent editions.

Unless otherwise acknowledged, all photographs are the property of Pearson Education, Inc.

Photo locators denoted as follows: Top (T), Center (C), Bottom (B), Left (L), Right (R), Background (Bkgd)

2 FSA/OWI Collection, Prints & Photographs Division, LC-DIG-ppmsc-00199/Library of Congress; 5 The George F. Landegger Collection of Alabama Photographs in Carol M. Highsmith's America, Prints & Photographs Division, LC-DIG-highsm-05751/ Library of Congress; 12 The George F. Landegger Collection of Alabama Photographs in Carol M. Highsmith's America, Prints & Photographs Division, LC-DIG-highsm-07060/Library of Congress.

ISBN-13: 978-0-328-67631-6
ISBN-10: 0-328-67631-4

15 16 17 18 17 16

Changing America

When Martin Luther King, Jr., was born in 1929, segregation was common in some parts of the United States. Under **segregation**, white and black people lived in different

A segregated waiting room

neighborhoods and attended separate schools.

Segregation meant that African American people were treated unfairly. Schools for African American children were usually inferior to those for white children. In some towns, there were no restaurants for them. In general, they did not have the same opportunities as white people. Often they were denied their **civil rights**, the rights all citizens have.

Segregation made many African American people deeply angry. Martin Luther King and others turned this anger into action and changed American history.

A Serious Student

King was born in a segregated neighborhood in Atlanta, Georgia. His father and his grandfather were pastors of a Baptist church. His parents hoped he would be a preacher, too. From boyhood, King heard powerful sermons. As a youngster, he learned to appreciate the power of words.

King was an intelligent, able student. He finished high school early and entered college when he was just 15 years old. The summer before college he worked on a farm in Connecticut. It was his first experience being in a place where the races weren't segregated. The experience opened his eyes and made him dislike segregation even more.

In college King studied religion and sociology, the science of human behavior. He graduated at the age of 19.

Martin Luther King, Jr., as a young boy (right) and his family

More Schooling

King continued his studies in Pennsylvania and later at Boston University in Massachusetts. Both colleges were **integrated**, which meant they had white and black students. King earned a doctorate in religious studies from Boston University. A doctorate is the highest level of learning that can be achieved. Now he was called Dr. King.

One of the things King studied was ways to change **society**. He learned about nonviolent, or peaceful, protest. He read about Mohandas Gandhi, who had practiced nonviolence in India. King didn't know then that he would be a leader in the battle for civil rights.

During his years of study, King also served as an assistant pastor at his father's church. In 1954, he became pastor of Dexter Avenue Baptist Church in Montgomery, Alabama.

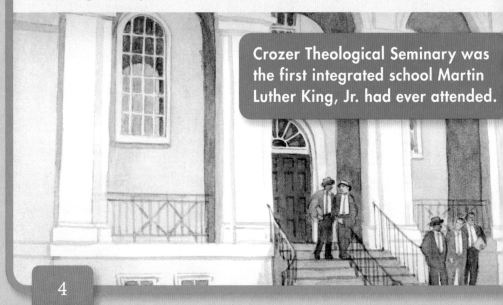

Crozer Theological Seminary was the first integrated school Martin Luther King, Jr. had ever attended.

An Arrest

Like most of the South, Montgomery was segregated. King hoped to work with other pastors, black and white, to change this and to enable all citizens to have equal civil rights. One thing they hoped to change was the situation on city buses.

When Martin Luther King, Jr. became pastor of Dexter Avenue Baptist Church, he was among the youngest pastors in Montgomery.

In Montgomery, as in many other southern cities, black and white people rode the same buses, but black riders were treated unfairly. They had to sit in the back. If there weren't enough seats for whites, black riders had to give up their seats.

On December 1, 1955, an African American woman named Rosa Parks got on a Montgomery city bus. More and more people got on, and the bus became crowded. Soon the bus driver ordered Parks to give her seat to a white rider. Parks refused. But the city law said black passengers had to surrender seats to white riders, so Parks was arrested.

A Decision

Word of Rosa Parks's arrest spread quickly in the black community. Community leaders, including King, met and discussed what to do. They decided to use the incident to try to change the bus segregation law. They decided on a one-day **boycott** of

Rosa Parks's arrest led to a bus boycott.

Montgomery city buses. They hoped city **officials** would see how unfair the laws were.

To make the boycott work, the pastors needed transportation for thousands of African Americans. In the 1950s, few of Montgomery's black citizens had cars. The pastors organized a car sharing system to replace bus rides. They handed out thousands of fliers that explained the boycott.

The boycott was set for December 5. Would it really work? That morning King and the other leaders watched. Thousands of Montgomery's black citizens stayed off the buses. Many walked to work or got rides from those who had cars. Across the city, empty city buses rolled from stop to stop!

A New Leader

That same day, boycott leaders decided that King should be their spokesperson. He was unsure if he was the right choice, but he accepted the job.

That evening, at a large meeting of thousands of Montgomery's black citizens, King proved it was the right decision. He spoke to the crowd. His powerful words inspired listeners to continue the boycott until city laws changed.

King's words hinted at what a great leader he would become. He said that black people weren't angry with white people, but they were angry with unfair laws. He said that black citizens wouldn't use violence to try to change the laws. They would use peaceful protest. He pointed out that black people were simply expecting to be treated like all other Americans. He also said that fighting for basic rights was part of American history. It was part of being an American. "If we are wrong," he said, "the Constitution of the United States is wrong!"

Every workday, tens of thousands of black Montgomery citizens normally rode buses.

Growing Tensions

The audience cheered King's words. There was great optimism at the meeting. The crowd left, determined to continue the bus boycott as long as it took. Yet danger was ahead. Could King's positive words keep the boycott peaceful?

There was reason to worry. King and other leaders were convinced that the boycott would work. Many white people supported it. In the early weeks of the boycott, many whites even drove African American citizens to work. Yet a great many whites were against civil rights for blacks. They were upset by change or perhaps afraid of it. White Montgomery officials decided to fight the boycott. Police arrested black drivers who gave boycotters rides. King himself was arrested.

As weeks went on, the boycott continued and tensions grew. The bus companies were upset that they were losing money. There was growing frustration in Montgomery. Soon, things got even worse.

Throughout the long bus boycott, cars and drivers were ready to help black citizens get to work.

A Life-Changing Night

King and the other leaders began to get death threats. Many of these came by phone. For King, the most significant threat came in late January 1956.

The boycott had already lasted more than six weeks and anger was growing in Montgomery. One evening, King's phone rang. It was yet another threat. This one made King especially anxious.

That night, King spent many sleepless hours confronting his fears. He was torn by worries about the safety of his family and himself. He also had deep concerns about the future of African Americans and all Americans as the fight for equality continued. He wondered if he should quit.

Finding Courage

King was also angry. He was angry at those who threatened him. He was angry with the white Montgomery officials who opposed the boycott, too. But he was determined not to give in to his anger. Instead he reminded himself that many whites supported the move for true equal rights among races. As for those who did not, King believed they would eventually change. They would recognize the unfairness of segregation.

In those dark, sleepless hours, King sat alone at his kitchen table and prayed. He prayed for the courage to ignore the danger to his own safety in the struggle ahead and for the courage to accept his own death. In the morning, he knew that both his bravery and his faith in a better America would not weaken no matter what risks he faced. King was armed with the courage he needed.

Tested

A few nights later, someone threw a bomb onto King's front porch. He wasn't home, but his wife Coretta and infant daughter, Yolanda, were there.

Word of the bombing quickly reached King. He rushed home to discover that his family was thankfully unharmed. He also discovered a large crowd of angry black citizens in front of his house. Some were armed and looking for revenge for the bombing.

King stood on his damaged porch and looked out at the angry crowd. In a calm, steady voice he said two things that he would repeat many times in the months ahead. The first was, "We cannot solve this problem with . . . violence. We must meet violence with nonviolence."

The second thing he said was that even if he were killed, the fight for civil rights would continue.

Martin Luther King, Jr. stood on his porch and asked people to remain calm.

An Inspiring Leader

That night, King's words helped calm the crowd. King's speech showed his decision to live without fear. It also showed his hopes of changing the ideas of people who disagreed with him. His words inspired the black community to continue the boycott and to fight with nonviolence, not weapons.

From his bombed porch, King showed all of America that his was a brave voice. Even a bombing would not stop him. The Montgomery bus boycott would continue. So would the broader battle for equal civil rights for all Americans. The next day, people all over America read about the calm and determined young leader.

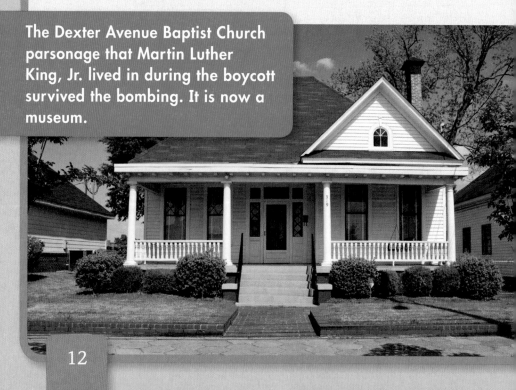

The Dexter Avenue Baptist Church parsonage that Martin Luther King, Jr. lived in during the boycott survived the bombing. It is now a museum.

The Fight Continues

The next day the boycott continued, and the buses stayed empty. Montgomery now understood something important. The black community would never give in to fear or violence.

The success of the Montgomery bus boycott was an important step in the long battle for racial equality in America.

That same day, African American lawyers went to court to fight the city's bus segregation laws. The court battles lasted almost a year. During that time King and other leaders were often arrested. More threats and real violence were directed at them, but the boycott went on. Day after day, week after week, thousands of people refused to board Montgomery city buses.

Finally the United States Supreme Court declared that Montgomery's bus segregation law was illegal. On December 21, 1956, a little over a year after it began, the boycott ended. The boycotters had won. African Americans rode the buses again, and they could sit in any seat they chose.

A National Leader

The boycott was just the start of King's fight for civil rights. In 1957, he and others started a new civil rights group called the Southern Christian Leadership Conference. Their goal was to end segregation in places such as restaurants, hotels, theaters, and schools. They also worked to guarantee all Americans the same voting rights.

Under King's leadership, the group fought many battles to end segregation. They did so without violence, by holding protest marches and boycotts.

In 1963, at a large rally in Washington, D.C., King spoke to more than 250,000 black and white people. He delivered a powerful speech called, "I Have a Dream." It is considered one of the greatest speeches in United States history.

Time line of Martin Luther King, Jr.'s Life

1929
Born in Atlanta on
January 15

1948
Enters the seminary to
become a Baptist minister

1930   1935   1940   1945

1951
Enters Boston University

King's Words Live On

Many of King's efforts were successful. His speeches changed minds and made Americans understand and support the need for civil rights for all. New laws improved the lives of many Americans. But the road wasn't easy. King faced constant threats, actual attacks, and frequent arrests. Still, he never gave into fear. He always carried the same message of hope.

In 1964, King was awarded the Nobel Peace Prize. He was the youngest person to receive the award, but on April 4, 1968, an **assassin** shot and killed Martin Luther King, Jr. Yet his words, and his message, live on.

1955
Montgomery bus boycott begins

1956
Supreme Court declares bus segregation illegal

1964
Receives the Nobel Peace Prize

1955   **1960**   **1965**   **1970**

1957
Starts Southern Christian leadership Conference

1963
Gives I Have a Dream speech in Washington, D.C.

1968
Is shot and killed in Memphis, Tennessee

15

Glossary

assassin someone who murders a leader or other important person

boycott to protest by not buying something or not using a service

civil rights the rights guaranteed to all citizens, such as equal treatment under the law

integrated not segregated

official a leader of a government or organization

segregation separating people because of race

society a community of people living under a set of laws

MARTIN LUTHER KING, JR.
and the
Struggle for Civil Rights

Dennis Fertig

Boston, Massachusetts
Chandler, Arizona
Glenview, Illinois
Upper Saddle River, New Jersey

Illustrations
Opener, 1, 3, 4, 6, 7, 8, 9, 10, 11, 13, 15 Bandelin-Dacey.

Photographs
Every effort has been made to secure permission and provide appropriate credit for photographic material.
The publisher deeply regrets any omission and pledges to correct errors called to its attention in subsequent editions.

Unless otherwise acknowledged, all photographs are the property of Pearson Education, Inc.

Photo locators denoted as follows: Top (T), Center (C), Bottom (B), Left (L), Right (R), Background (Bkgd)

2 FSA/OWI Collection, Prints & Photographs Division, LC-DIG-ppmsc-00199/Library of Congress; 5 The George F. Landegger Collection of Alabama Photographs in Carol M. Highsmith's America, Prints & Photographs Division, LC-DIG-highsm-05751/ Library of Congress; 12 The George F. Landegger Collection of Alabama Photographs in Carol M. Highsmith's America, Prints & Photographs Division, LC-DIG-highsm-07060/Library of Congress.

ISBN-13: 978-0-328-67631-6
ISBN-10: 0-328-67631-4

15 16 17   18 17 16